I0489872

The Smart Business guide to Health Care Reform
(Including the Effect of the Employer Mandate Delay)

© Kevin J. Rejent 2013

Author: Kevin J. Rejent

www.rejentfirm.com

First Edition: August 2013

To my wife Lori, daughters Amelia and Charlotte, and twin boys coming any day now, thank you for your patience and inspiration.

TABLE OF CONTENTS

Section 1 – How Did We Get Here?

Section 4 – Gazing Into the Crystal Ball

Introduction

It's The Law, It's Not Going Away,
So You Probably Want to Follow It.

Health Care Reform, HCR, PPACA, ACA, Obamacare, Socialized Medicine, the Greatest Thing Since Sliced Bread. Whatever you want to call it and however you feel about it, all that matters is that the Supreme Court upheld it, voters refused to kill it by electing a new President, and while the Employer Mandate has been delayed, opponents in Congress are powerless to stop it. Even with the gift of a one year delay of the Employer Mandate, all of the energy you spent vigorously ignoring it while hoping it went away or got much simpler was for naught. And now employees are nervous, your renewal is near, and every day, you hear something new that sounds important, but you just don't know where to mentally file that compliance strategy or requirement you just heard.

The Patient Protection and Affordable Care Act is complicated, and regardless of whether your company employs one or one-hundred thousand, it directly impacts your business's current and future health insurance. If you are responsible for making these decisions for your company, more likely than not, it is also causing stress and anxiety that is also impacting your personal well-being, as well. Like all laws, however, it is manageable when you are able to determine what portions impact you and concentrating on those issues.

Short of reading and understanding the entire law and all corresponding regulations (over 10,000 pages by some estimates), there is no way to definitively state exactly what provisions are applicable to you. However, who, other than insurance professionals and attorneys who enjoy being tortured by regulations, has time to keep up?

What this book IS:

This book is your short cut to understanding what PPACA says, what it doesn't say, and how both will impact your business. The purpose is not to tell you everything about the law; but rather to inform you of the relevant provisions and translate those provisions from bureaucrat-speak to plain English. So while you may not fully understand how the Department of Justice and Federal Trade Commission will apply antitrust laws to Accountable Care Organizations,[1] you hopefully *will* have the tools you need to assess your organization's exposure to key aspects of PPACA.

What this book IS NOT:

First and foremost, this book is not a legal treatise. Nobody enjoys reading statutory provisions followed by case citations in response to basic questions regarding massive changes in law that impact everyone. Statutory and regulatory citations will be avoided whenever possible and any bureaucrat-speak that cannot be avoided will be translated.

Similarly, this book is not legal, accounting, or insurance advice. While I hope you find all of the information useful and applicable to your organization, it is not written specifically to advise anyone regarding any specific individual question. The goal is to put you in a position to intelligently discuss your options with your insurance advisor, accountant, and/or attorney.

Finally, this book is not an op-ed piece. If you are looking for a book to rail against the commie proponents of the law and say inflammatory things about alleged death panels, keep looking. Similarly, if you want to read flowery love notes about increased access to care and improved benefits, sorry, this book is not for you, either. While an occasional opinion may

---

[1] In fairness, nobody does.

slip in here or there to lighten up what can be a rather dry subject matter (see footnote 1), the purpose of the book is to help you understand and comply with the law. Regardless of your opinion of the law, IT IS THE LAW, and last I checked, the Supreme Court has not yet exempted people who don't like a particular law from complying with it. It's here, it's not going anywhere anytime soon, and loving or hating it does not impact the degree to which you must be in compliance.

Book Structure

To make this book as useful as possible, it is broken into sections addressing different topics. Within each section, there are chapters. Those chapters have a discussion of the important law regarding a certain element of the law. Each chapter concludes with "Take Away Points" that give a bullet-point summary of the chapter, followed by "Action Items" suggesting steps you can take to evaluate how your business is handling or can handle the issue. Finally, there is an area for notes after each set of Action Items for you to jot down things to do in response to what you read, such as "call broker to discuss" or "find out what HR is doing."

This law fundamentally changes how Americans obtain their health insurance and employers' responsibilities related to that change. It is difficult to understand with many moving targets, grandiose goals, undefined standards, and enflamed rhetoric on all sides. However, you *can* understand it. You *can* learn what matters for your business. Most important, your organization *can* weather the storm and succeed in complying with the law while remaining focused on your primary business objectives.

SECTION 1 – HOW DID WE GET HERE?

Chapter 1: They Passed the Law, Now We Get to Find Out What Is In It.

On Christmas Eve 2009, The United States Senate gave the nation either, depending on your perspective, a great Christmas gift or a lump of coal by approving its version of PPACA.[2] This was one of the myriad of crucial legislative acts in this drama, including Massachusetts electing a Republican Senator (yes, Massachusetts) and Senate Majority Leader Harry Reid invoking the reconciliation process, that resulted the President Obama signing the bill into law on March 23, 2010.

Along the way, House Speaker Nancy Pelosi famously told a crowd that Representatives "have to pass the bill, so [the nation] can find out what's in it." Well, the bill passed, and we have spent the last three-plus years learning what is in it and learning what bureaucrats at the Internal Revenue Service, Department of Labor, and Department of Health and Human Services think is in it by the regulations they have promulgated. This book is the guide to "what's in it."

But before we discuss the regulations regarding how to compute the impact of seasonal employees on your full-time equivalent calculation, HSA changes, or any of the other technical compliance issues, understanding the "big picture" of the law may help us understand the rationale for some of the technical issues.

Title I – Quality, Affordable Healthcare for All Americans

Well that sounds nice! Who is against that?

---

[2] I will refer to the law as PPACA or ACA instead of the somewhat politically charged and derisive "Obamacare."

This is the meat of the law impacting employers and, as you may have guessed, is not *quite* as agreeable as its name suggests. This title contains such important provisions as:

- Prohibition against lifetime limits to coverage and discrimination against those with pre-existing conditions;
- Guaranteed issue and community rating;
- Essential Health Benefits;
- Benefits Exchanges;
- Individual and small business tax credits;
- The Individual Mandate;
- The Employer Mandate
- And much, MUCH more.

Since these topics will be discussed at length throughout this book, the 30,000 foot understanding of this title for right now is that its drafters were intending to make coverage easier to get, harder to lose, and of some certain quality.

Title II – Getting More People Into Government Programs

OK, that is not *really* the name given to this title, but I think everyone can agree it is more helpful in understanding the purpose of this portion of the law than the innocuous "Role of Public Programs." This section provides full federal funding for several years, tapered down to 90% of the costs of expansion, to states for expanding Medicaid eligibility to all non-elderly citizens with incomes at or below 133% of the Federal Poverty Level.

This was non-negotiable until the Supreme Court ruled states could choose whether or not they would accept the terms of the federal government's offer. (More on that later.) Of course, the goal was to get more people insured through a program of a quality the government could certainly approve because it is their own program.

Through two titles, you may be sensing a theme. And if you are thinking to yourself "expanding coverage is one thing, but shouldn't we be concerned about controlling costs?", then pat yourself on the back, because you just anticipated:

Title III – Improving the Quality and Efficiency of Health Care

While the first two titles were primarily concerned with getting people insured, this title wants to lower the cost of health care. Government cannot set the rates private insurers pay doctors and hospitals, but it does have a very large stick with the ability to set Medicare rates. Most insurers base their reimbursement rate to providers on some amount over the Medicare reimbursement rate. Thus, the theory goes, but lowering the amount Medicare spends on services, the government is also lowering the amount private insurers spend on services.

In an effort to lower Medicare costs, the law attempts to link payment to the quality of the outcome, not the quantity of services provided. This is not a new approach, as HMOs have been trying to do it for decades. The difference is that the government has much more contracting leverage than individual HMOs, and can (in theory) dictate that providers accept the payment model the government imposes on them. Some of the means by which the government attempts to reach its goals are: Accountable Care Organizations ("ACOs"), improved medical billing coding, the Independent Payment Advisory Board ("IPAB") (the body Sarah Palin famously labeled "Death Panels"), and various community health initiatives.

Title IV – Keeping People From Getting Sick

Again, this is not the "official" title, but is more descriptive than its dull given name.[3] And for a business perspective, the only take away is that the law funds public health programs in the hopes that fewer people get sick, and thus fewer people use medical resources.

Title V – Health Care Workforce

Thus far, the law has attempted to greatly add to the number of people who can access medical services and attempted to limit the amount providers will be paid for providing those services. Isn't the average medical student $160,000-$210,000 in debt at the time of their graduation? Now you want them to care for more patients for less money?

Realizing some incentives may be necessary to get medical professionals into the expanded system, this title attempts to soften the blow of the cost of medical school, especially for those who go into primary care medicine. It also expands the role nurses play in our system by loosening some of the requirements for nurse practitioners and subsidizing some nursing education.

Is this enough to counter the disincentives other portions of the law create? See Introduction – "What This Book *is Not*" – an op-ed piece. We'll let the economists among us provide that opinion.

Titles VI-IIX and X – Stuff That Has Been Repealed, Has No Real Impact on Businesses, and/or Very Few People Outside of the Health Care Provision Industry Care About

---

[3] If you must know, it is "Prevention of Chronic Disease and Improving Public Health."

Again, I may be taking minor liberties with the official titles, but you get the idea.

Title IX – Revenue Provisions

You knew there had to be a bill somewhere in here, and they stuck it towards the end between titles you would need to be specifically looking for, hoping readers' eyes were glossed over by this point. This title seeks to raise money for the law's various pet projects through:

- Tax on "Cadillac plans,"
- Higher tax on non-qualifying HSA and MSA distributions;
- Limitations on Flex Spending Accounts;
- Fee on prescription drug manufacturers and importers;
- Tax on medical devices;
- Tax on insurance plans;
- Elimination of Medicare Part D expense deductions;
- Tax increase on "high-income earners;"
- Excise tax on elective cosmetic surgeries;
- And many more fees and taxes.

There are a lot of new programs, tax credits, and expansion and modifications of established programs in this bill. As you can imagine, this costs money…a lot of money. At the time of writing, Uncle Sam is not particularly flush with extra cash, so the money needs to come from somewhere, and the American people would not have stood for higher income taxes. So the drafters are attempting to look under every proverbial couch cushion they can identity for the funds necessary to operate the new programs. Will it be enough to cover costs without raising income taxes? We'll again defer to the economists and leave that thermonuclear issue to more partisan authors.

TAKE AWAY POINTS

- The primary goal of the law is to ensure an acceptable level of health insurance coverage by the most people possible through either private insurance or government programs.
- Government cannot set the rates private insurers pay to providers, but attempts to lower those rates by adjusting Medicare reimbursements.
- There are several tax increases and fees in the law because the law almost certainly would not have passed if it relied upon an income tax increase for funding.

ACTION ITEMS

- Attempt to filter any new information you hear about health care reform by the various sections and understand that several of the sections (and thus much of the new information) does not impact your business.

NOTES

_____

_____

_____

Chapter 2 - So What did the Supreme Court Do Again?

It's Constitutional, but Not for Any of the Reasons Anyone Thought It Would Be

If anyone claims they predicted the Supreme Court would uphold PPACA based upon Congressional taxing authority, they are a) lying, or b) really, really lying. This aspect of the decision, which saved the law from the teeth of unconstitutionality, is still hotly contested. How did the Court get there, and what else did the Court say that effects application of the law? Staying true to this book's stated goal of NOT being a legal treatise, please accept the following as "The Non-Lawyers Legal Jargon-Free Guide to Understanding the Supreme Court's Health Care Reform Opinion."

As the case was making its way through the courts and before the Supreme Court issued an opinion, the primary questions were: 1) is the Individual Mandate (the provision requiring everyone to buy health insurance) proper under the Commerce Clause and 2) would the Court allow the rest of the law to stand if the Individual Mandate was killed. The Commerce Clause gives Congress the power to regulate commerce between the states. Thus, if economic activity relates to two states or crosses state lines, Congress can regulate it, and the Supreme Court has been very deferential to Congress when determining what can be regulated under this Congressional authority. However, in this case, Congress was attempting to regulate the economic *inactivity* of failing to buy insurance under the theory that it hurt those who do buy insurance. The government argued the Individual Mandate was essential to the success of the entire system...until it appeared the Court might strike down the Mandate, at which time the government said it wasn't that big a deal, and law would be fine without it.

The government also argued that Congress has the power to levy taxes and, although the bill's supporters went to great lengths to portray the money paid as a fine, not a tax, it was a tax. Opponents claimed the Medicaid expansion contained in the bill was an abuse of Congressional Spending Powers. Neither of these arguments was taken seriously because their historic track record was abysmal.

Guess which arguments won?

The Court ruled, much to the delight of the law's opponents, that Congress could not justify the law under the Commerce Clause. Additionally, and further exciting the opponents, the Court ruled that the federal government could not require states to expand Medicaid. Thus, states were given a choice of whether they wanted to accept the terms of the government's deal or decline. As you may recall, one of the primary purposes of the law was to expand the number of people covered in either private or government plans, so this was a major blow.

If you are an opponent of the law, you are breaking out the party hats right now.

Hold on.

Keep reading.

Chief Justice Roberts, applying a Supreme Court judicial review theory that states a law should be upheld if there is *any* reason to uphold it, went searching for a reason. He hadn't looked far before he noticed that the whole "it's a tax" argument was right in front of the Court. It took some contortion, but he made the theory fit the case, and found four other justices to sign on, saving the law from an historic defeat.[4] So while the

----

[4] In reality, the four justices who agreed with Chief Justice Roberts would have

law's supporters lost on every important issue, they won the case; and the law's opponents were given the "moral victory" of being right on every issue, but the ultimate losers.

So We're All Finished with the Court Challenges, Right?

Ha!

The case decided by the Supreme Court was what is referred to as a "facial challenge," which means the challengers claimed the law, no matter how it is applied, could never be constitutional. The Court said, no, it is not, on its face, unconstitutional.

That leaves "as applied" challenges, which seek to have a particular application of a law, or portion of a law, declared unconstitutional. These are favored by Courts because, unlike a facial challenge that requires the Court to guess in absolutist terms whether the law could ever be constitutional, an as applied challenge uses real events to show how evil and unconstitutional the particular challenged law is. There are *plenty* of "as applied" lawsuits lurking in the thousands of pages of the law and its regulations, just waiting to be triggered by some well-intentioned Department of Labor or IRS bureaucrat. While none likely have the ability to kill the entire law like the challenge to the Individual Mandate had, it is safe to say the government will have its hands full for the next several years defending this law. We will discuss some of these potential issues later in the book, but will barely scratch the surface of all of the potential suits. So in addition to handling the massive, forward-looking implementation of an enormous overhaul of one-fifth of our economy, the IRS, Department of Labor, and Health and Human Services

---

agreed to *any* reason that would save the law...taxing authority, Commerce Clause, color of the Solicitor General's socks...anything.

will also be required to look back and defend every action they take in implementation. That'll be fun.

TAKE AWAY POINTS

- The Court found the Individual Mandate constitutional as an exercise of Congressional Taxing Authority.
- The law's opponents won on the "big" issue, the Commerce Clause, but lost the case.
- Mandatory Medicaid expansion cannot be justified by the Spending Clause, and thus, states have the right to decline to participate.
- We have not seen the last of lawsuits challenging PPACA.

ACTION ITEMS

- Pay attention to new PPACA lawsuits to determine if they may impact your business.

NOTES

_____

_____

_____

_____

Chapter 3 – Why Are Premiums Rising?

Knowing what the law says and what the Supreme Court decided are great and can impress people at dinner parties; but the question that may be on your mind at this point is: what about this law is causing health insurance premiums to increase?

Is PPACA the Problem?

Supporters of the law note (correctly) that premiums have generally been increasing for the past decade, and PPACA slows the acceleration of these increases. However, the generally-accepted theory, even among the law's supporters, is that certain elements of this law will apply upward pressure to premiums. The extent the upward pressure may increase premiums and whether other elements of the law meant to remedy the potential increases will offset this pressure are questions best left for the actuaries among us. This chapter is intended to explain to those who believe premiums are increasing what about this law could possibly cause those increases.

Community Rating/Age Bands

It is axiomatic that those who present the lowest risk to insurance companies pay the lowest rates, and those who present the highest risk pay the highest rates. This is why a teenaged boy driving a sports car is more expensive to insure than a 40 year-old mother driving a minivan, and homeowners next to a consistently-flooded river pay more than their neighbors on a hill a few miles away. Health insurance is no different.

The health insurance equivalents of the 40 year old minivan mom or homeowner on a hill are the "young invincibles." These 20-something males are healthy, rarely use medical resources, and barely ever need a prescription for anything other than basic antibiotics. Since they are such a low risk to submit claims, they are relatively cheap to insure, and insurers want to get them in the system, at any low price, because the insurer will almost certainly make a profit on them.

The teenage hot-rodders or river-bank homeowners of health insurance are older individuals who have not quite reached Medicare age, but see doctors frequently for chronic issues and take lots of pills. As you can imagine based upon their increased use of medical resources and increased risk to the insurer of submitting claims, insurers need to charge them more so as not to lose money by insuring them.

Insurers use what are called "age bands" to determine how much more they will charge the older, greater risk customers than the younger, lower risk customers. According to the America's Health Insurance Plans, forty-two states presently have age bands of 5:1 or higher,[5] and several states have age-bands of up to 9:1. In oversimplified terms, that means if a low-risk customer is paying $100/month in a plan with a 5:1 age band, a high-risk customer is paying $500/month. The insurer then hopes that these two customers combine for less than $600 in claims in a month so it can make a profit.

Regulators attempt to control age bands by implementing "community rating," which means everyone in the same community must be provided the same rate, regardless of age, gender, sex, race, medical history, or tobacco use. Most community rating laws are "modified

---

[5] America's Health Insurance Plans, *Age Rating,* available at: http://ahip.org/Issues/Age-Rating.aspx (last visited July 17, 2013).

community rating" regulations because they will permit some variance, especially with respect to age and tobacco use.

PPACA contains a modified community rating regulation for the individual and small-group (less than 50 lives) markets that requires insurers to apply an age band of, at most, 3:1.[6] Thus, if the insurer is charging the low-risk customer $100/month, it can only charge the high-risk customer $300/month. Even without pretending to understand very much about actuarial science, it is easy to see how this could cause rates to rise. Instead of keeping the lowest rate at $100/month, the insurer might raise the rates of the low-risk customers to bring them up to the 3:1 age band and increase the probability that all of the submitted claims will be covered by the participants' combined premium payments.

Guaranteed Issue

Well then, won't the insurers simply choose wisely who they insure? They would if they could, but the law contains a provision called "guaranteed issue," which means they must insure all comers, regardless of age, sex, health history, or any other underwriting criteria. Some call this the ban on pre-existing conditions denials, and it is, but it is much more.

While guaranteed issue is a blessing for those with pre-existing conditions, when combined with community rating, it creates a very tricky situation for insurers who need to figure out how to offer an affordable product that will still make money. Traditional underwriting is significantly hampered (some would argue this is a good thing) and pricing could be more of a guess than projection.

This acceptance of all applicants also means someone can pay the Individual Mandate tax (or penalty…whatever you want to call it) until

6 Insurers may also charge smokers 1.5 times the rate of non-smokers.

---

they need medical services, then buy insurance. Because the tax will likely be less than the premium, there is a real concern among insurers that the only Young Invincibles they will get will be those who recently found out they are not so invincible and need care.

Essential Health Benefits

Fine, so insurers are limited in the amount they can vary rates between customers and must offer coverage to everyone. The obvious answer is to water down the coverage and/or require a very high deductible, right?

The law's drafters figured you would say that (you sneaky fox), and ended that conversation before it began. In order for a plan to be of sufficient quality to avoid the employer mandate penalty, it must include Essential Health Benefits contained in a selected state "Benchmark Plan."

The law requires ten categories of coverage be included in every plan:

1. Ambulatory patient services

2. Emergency services

3. Hospitalization

4. Maternity and newborn care

5. Mental health and substance use disorder services, including behavioral health treatment

6. Prescription drugs

7. Rehabilitative and habilitative services and devices

18

8. Laboratory services

9. Preventive and wellness services and chronic disease management, and

10. Pediatric services, including oral and vision care

The key aspect of each Benchmark Plan for the purposes of this discussion is that its deductible must be no higher than $2,000.00 for an individual or $4,000.00 for a family.

Ban on Annual and Lifetime Limits

"Wow, so there really aren't many opportunities to rein in costs," you may be thinking to yourself, "at least most plans contain annual and lifetime limits." Not anymore.

Beginning in 2014, plans may no longer place annual or lifetime limitations on the essential health benefits. They may still limit benefits that are not considered essential, but plans will have so few of these that the risk of hitting limits would be pretty low.

Provisions to Lower Premiums

Understanding that some of the law's mandates might tend to increase premiums, the drafters included a few provisions intended to lower them. First, it requires any insurer seeking to increase premiums more than 10% to justify those rates before a state or federal commission. However, the commissions have no authority to deny the rate increase, only determine if they are justified.

The law also seeks to lower Medicare reimbursements to providers. Medicare rates, as you may recall, are often the basis for rates paid by private health insurance companies to providers. Thus, by decreasing Medicare rates, the government would likely also decrease cost to private insurers.

The biggest experiments in cost controls, however, are the exchanges. We will discuss these in more detail in Chapter 8, but the general theory is that the exchanges will lower costs by dramatically increasing the size of the group, thus giving it more leverage.

TAKE AWAY POINTS

- Premium increases were occurring for several years before PPACA became the law.
- Community Rating, Guaranteed Issue, Essential Health Benefits, and the ban on annual and lifetime limits are causing upward pressure on premiums.
- It is too early to determine if government efforts to lessen this upward pressure through rate reviews, Medicare payment reductions, and the exchanges will be effective.

ACTION ITEMS

- Read newspaper and magazine articles and watch news stories regarding the topics discussed in this chapter as possibly driving up premiums.
- Begin thinking about your plan. Does it have a high deductible or annual/lifetime limits? Will it need to be changed to comply with the law?

NOTES

_____

_____

_____

So there you have it. You now know what the law says, what the Supreme Court said about the law, and why the law may be driving up premiums. You are now sufficiently prepared to dive into the law and get your hands dirty with the details you need to ensure your company's plan complies with the law in the most cost-effective manner possible.

SECTION 2 - EMPLOYER RESPONSIBILITIES

Chapter 4 – The Employer Mandate

Employers everywhere rejoiced when the Treasury Department (parent of the IRS) announced that the Employer Mandate, which was scheduled to take effect in 2014, would be delayed until 2015. Specifically, it delayed employers' and insurers' obligation to report if coverage was offered and the specifics of that coverage.

Setting aside the question of whether it had the authority to do this without the approval of Congress, this action changed employers' calculations regarding their insurance offerings. Some are viewing it as a "free year" and cutting benefits without penalties; others are using it as a practice year to see if some aggressive plans will satisfy the Mandate when penalties are assessed; and others are making no changes, figuring there are plenty of reasons to offer insurance. What must be kept in mind is that the Employer Mandate did not go away, it is merely delayed. And even more important: all other aspects of the law (guaranteed issue, community rating, etc.) still take full effect on January 1, 2014, so "the law" was not delayed, just this one part.

For those interested in preparing for the Employer Mandate, the first thing to know about it is whether your company is even affected by the Employer Mandate. If the answer is "no," then while there are plenty of PPACA provisions that will impact your coverage, this isn't one of them. If you are subject to the mandate, knowing the result of all courses of action, including paying the penalty, will allow you to make the best decision for your organization.

Does the Law Apply to You?

The two statements most commonly uttered regarding whether the Employer Mandate applies to a particular organization are:

"If you don't have 50 full-time employees, you don't have to worry about it."

"If you have more than 50 employees, even part-timers, you have to worry about it."

Both are right, and both are wrong. The confusion stems from the law's use of "full-time equivalent" in the formula calculating whether the mandate applies, and "full time employees" in the formula used to calculate the penalty if coverage is not offered. First, the focus is on whether the mandate applies, so full time equivalent is the important phrase; but what the heck is a "full-time equivalent" employee?! Some definitions are in order:

- Full-time employee (FTEm) – In general, this is any worker who works an average of 30 hours per week or more during a particular measurement period or is hired with the assumption that they will work 30 hours or more per week. (We'll address those measurement periods in Chapter 6).

- Full-time equivalent employees (FTEq) – The number you arrive at by taking the total number of hours worked by part-time (less than 30 hour/week) employees in a month divided by 120 (hours a 30-hour per week full time employee would work in a month).

  o For example, if you have 10 employees averaging 15 hours per week, your part time employees have worked 600 hours, and are considered 5 "full time equivalent" employees for the purposes of this calculation.

Thus, the formula to determine if your company is subject to the Employer Mandate is simply:

FTEm + FTEq

If that number is less than 50, WOO-HOO! No Mandate for you!

If that number is greater than 50, you get to move onto the next step: figuring out the various penalties you could be subject to in certain circumstance.

Play or Pay

If you have fifty or more employees, congratulations on being successful enough to employ so many people, but there are some additional responsibilities that come with that status. You are subject to the mandate; but what does that mean? What kind of penalty are you really looking at if you decide not to provide coverage to your employees?[7]

It is important to note that, unlike the formula we used to determine whether or not you are subject to the Mandate, we only care about *real, honest to goodness full time employees* here. And to give employers on the smaller side of the group subject to the Mandate a break, the law does not require companies to pay a penalty on the first 30 employees. So an employer over 50 employees must pay a penalty of $2000/per employee after the first 30 if it does not offer insurance.[8] Accordingly, the formula is:

(FTEm − 30) x $2,000 = Play or Pay Penalty

For example, if you have 50 full time employees (regardless of how many full time equivalent employees you have), your calculation

---

[7] You actually only need to offer insurance to 95% of your full time employees to avoid the penalty, so enjoy figuring out the 5% who are not offered it, and make sure their exclusion is not discriminatory under ERISA. Good luck with that. Or you could just offer it to 100% of your full-time employees.

[8] In order for the penalty to apply, at least one employee must seek a tax credit to purchase health insurance in an exchange. Assume at least one will if no coverage is offered.

would by: (50-30) x $2,000 = $40,000 penalty if you fail to offer insurance.

Unaffordable/Low Quality Coverage Penalty

What if you offer insurance to your full time employees, but it costs the employee a large chunk of their income to participate and/or it, for lack of a better term, stinks? There is a different, higher per employee penalty for that. Fret not, though, because although this penalty is $3,000.00 per full time employee for which it is charged, it can never be higher than the penalty would be if the organization did not offer insurance at all.

Coverage is deemed unaffordable if the employee's share of the premium[9] exceeds 9.5% of their household income. How the heck is the employer supposed to know the employee's household income? The regulations suggest the employer should just assume that the pay from that employer is the total household income. Further, if the employee is hourly with variable hours, an employee contribution of less than 9.5% of the Federal Poverty Level will be deemed acceptable.

Coverage is considered "low quality" if it does not meet actuarial value of 60%, which roughly means that the plan must cover at least 60% of the total allowed costs. What are "total allowed costs" and how is "actuarial value" calculated? Just leave that to the insurance companies and get their verification that it meets minimum requirements. There is absolutely no reason your company should try to figure this out…unless you are a company of actuaries, in which case, have at it.

If the organization's plan fails one of these tests, it is not automatically penalized. One of its employees would need to decline the

[9] For individual coverage, not family.

coverage offered by the company and apply for a tax credit to be used to purchase health insurance through whatever exchange is operational in that state. For each employee that seeks a tax credit, the organization will be charged a $3000.00 penalty. However, as noted above, the organization's total penalty may not exceed what the penalty would have been had the organization not offered insurance at all.

I Have a GREAT Idea!

Let me guess: this idea involves either moving everyone to part time or breaking the organization up into multiple companies, none of which would be subject to the Employer Mandate. Let me save you the time – don't.

As discussed above, the initial calculation used to determine if the Employer Mandate applies to an organization takes all employees into account. Moving people to part time would likely only save the amount of the penalty, not move your organization from one to which the Mandate applies to one that it does not. Additionally, ERISA established safeguards to protect employees from losing coverage through schemes like this. A company *may* be able to justify it, but the money it would spend defending the actions might eat up the savings, and the risk of losing a lawsuit filed by an aggrieved employee should be strongly considered.

Similarly, breaking the company into smaller companies will likely cost more than the potential savings and almost certainly not help the company avoid the Employer Mandate. The IRS will use the "control test" to determine if the companies are, in fact, separate companies or just a ruse to avoid the Mandate. Keys facts it will look for are to whom the new company was sold or transferred, who has actual control of the company, whether the companies file a tax return as affiliated companies, and whether the spin off had a "legitimate business purpose." As you can surely imagine, the IRS does not consider avoiding the Employer Mandate a "legitimate business purpose." If it sees a company broken into several companies after PPACA was passed, all of which *just* miss being subject to the Employer Mandate, red flags will be raised in IRS offices from Honolulu to Bangor. Organizations that try this scheme, and there will be plenty, will be the proverbial "low hanging fruit" that will easily be made examples of by the government.

TAKE AWAY POINTS

- The Employer Mandate has been delayed from 2014 to 2015, but has not been stricken from the law.
- The Employer Mandate applies to organizations with fifty (50) or more full time equivalent employees.
- Calculate full time equivalents by multiplying the number hours worked by part time employees in a month and divide by 120, then add that number to the number of actual full time employees (over 30 hours/week) working for the organization. If that number is greater than 50, the Employer Mandate applies.
- The penalty if no coverage is offered is equal to $2000.00 multiplied by the number of actual full time employees (not full time equivalents) minus thirty.
- A $3000.00 penalty is charged for each full time employee that seeks coverage through a health insurance exchange if the coverage offered by the employer is either unaffordable or low quality.

- Moving everyone to part time or breaking up the company to avoid the Employer Mandate are very risky and should not be undertaken without careful guidance from an attorney and accountant.

ACTION ITEMS

- Use the formula above to determine if the Employer Mandate applies to your organization.
- Calculate the various penalties and write down the amounts so that you can discuss all of your options with your insurance agent, accountant, and/or attorney.
- Make sure your insurance plan meets minimum value so you are not tripped up by the low quality plan penalty.
- Consult with an attorney and/or accountant before moving employees to part time or breaking a company into smaller companies.

NOTES

_____

_____

_____

_____

Chapter 5 – Why Offer Insurance at All?

After computing your potential penalties and comparing those numbers to your premiums, you may be wondering why you would continue to offer health insurance as an employee benefit. Why not just get out of the insurance business and save yourself the headache, especially since the delay of the Employer Mandate basically gives employers a "free year"? This chapter will show you that the decision is not as easy as it seems because the savings are not as great as you may think, and there are several business reasons to continue to provide coverage.

Penalties are Not Tax Deductible

Health insurance premiums paid by employers are tax deductible to the employer (and the employee's portion is deductible to him or her). Thus, $100 of pre-tax dollar spending is the equivalent of $130 in post-tax dollar spending if the tax rate is 30%.

The penalties are not tax deductible, so the employer would be paying it with post-tax dollars. Accordingly, if the employer's penalty is $100,000.00 and its tax rate is 30%, that is the equivalent of applying $130,000.00 towards premiums. The employer should also factor in increased accounting and/or legal fees if the penalty is charged. So the savings may not be as great as they first appear.

Giving Raises Equal to Exchange Coverage Costs

Some employers who want to make sure their employees are taken care of, but also want to get out of the insurance business, are contemplating offering raises equal to the amount an employee will need to spend to obtain coverage in an exchange. This plan, however, does not always lead to the savings the employer had anticipated.

Brokers and insurance consultants have amazing computer programs that can assist organizations in determining the true financial impact (not even taking into account the employee relations impact) of discontinuing coverage and providing raises sufficient to purchase comparable insurance in an exchange. First, the employer pays the penalty, and, as discussed above, the penalty is not tax deductible, so the true cost is really about 130% of the penalty. Then, determine the amount it will cost for each of the employees to obtain coverage for the same number of people currently in the plan provided by the employer (individual, family, etc.) in an exchange. Factor in any tax credits or subsidies the employee will be eligible for to reduce the amount of the raise they would need. Finally, add all of the employees together to determine the employer's "savings." While some employers still come out ahead, it is amazing how often the expecting "savings" can turn into a loss.

Business Value of Retaining Coverage

As more employers cut coverage and alter plans, health insurance will be a critical front in the war to attract and retain talent in the next several years. Workers will seek the security of employer sponsored coverage over the uncertainty of individual insurance purchased either in the private market or exchanges. Of course, low skilled or employees with skills that are easily replaced have less leverage, but is that who you are concerned about retaining or attracting?

Like always, those employees with skills of value to more than one employer will be able to command a better deal than other employees. In the past, that has traditionally meant more pay. In the future, however, it is feasible to assume some of these talented individuals will favor employers who offer health insurance even if the pay is slightly less than a competitor.

Think of those in your organization who bring a special skill to the group that other employers would love to have. Think about those employees' specific circumstances (age, family, general health, etc.) and ask yourself if they would bolt to a competitor if you stopped offering health insurance, even for less pay.

Now think of employees that you would like to work for your organization. How much easier would it be to attract them if their employer stopped offering health insurance? Would the value they bring to the organization exceed the cost of the health insurance provided?

We are likely several years away from businesses and the public at large having some level of comfort with the changes PPACA is bringing to our health insurance system. Until then, the health insurance cards employees receive from employers who still offer insurance will be treated like they are pure gold.

Employee Relations and Morale

While attracting and retaining talent is a primary reason to continue offering health insurance, maintaining employee morale and ensuring everyone is focused on doing their jobs to their fullest potential is an obvious benefit, as well. If an employee does not have health insurance, it is a pretty safe bet that the employee will spend a considerable amount of time, including time on the employer's dime, looking for a job that does offer insurance. Conversely, it is reasonable to assume that an employee with health insurance will be happy to remain with their present employer, even if they may be able to make more money elsewhere at a job without health insurance.

There are also potential employee relations problems that can turn into financial problems in the worst case scenarios. A broker in St. Louis uses a difficult, but not outlandish, hypothetical to drive the point home:

> Take Willie the custodian (it could be Willie the custodian, Susie the cafeteria lady, or Fred the Security guard, it doesn't matter.) Willie has been working for your company for thirty years. Everyone knows Willie, and everyone loves Willie; which is good, because Willie loves everyone right back. Willie works hard, does a good job, and even has a few people working under him. He is a model employee.
>
> One day, Willie doesn't feel so good and goes to the ER. There, they discover a spot on his lung that turns out to be cancer. The company had stopped providing insurance, instead giving each employee a raise to help them get coverage on their own. Unfortunately, Willie had a history of smoking and a few other issues, so even with the raise and tax credit, he couldn't get an affordable plan in the exchange. And he figured he was 63, so almost eligible for Medicare. His plan was to just stay healthy another year and a half. Even after he got sick, he could not afford the premiums in the exchange despite guaranteed issue and community rating because he has gone deep into debt trying to put two kids through college.
>
> So now Willie, the man everyone loves, has no insurance and no way to pay for the very expensive treatment he needs. Sure, you agree to pay him for the time off, but now his wife is calling asking if there is some way to get him insured again. Employees are asking what YOU are going to do for Willie. Even the upper level management who was on board with ceasing to

offer insurance is asking what the company is
going to do to take care of Willie.

What ARE you going to do? Pay for his
treatment? Take up a collection? Pay HIS
premiums in the exchange but nobody else's
(which could raise all sorts of discrimination and
tax issues)?

Of course, this is a very dramatic scenario, but not completely
unreasonable. It is easy to see how individual medical situations could
become employee relations nightmares very quickly.

Employee Health

Every business benefits from a healthy workforce. Having
employees in an employer sponsored health plan provides the employer
with the best opportunity to help create and maintain a healthy workforce.
The employer can implement wellness programs (which, we'll see Chapter
10, can lower premiums), work with a single insurer to develop a plan for
workplace health initiatives, and promote healthy behaviors through one
agent (the insurer).

If employees are spread out among several plans unaffiliated with
the company, the employer has no control over what types of wellness
programs employees are or (more likely) are not participating in.
Additionally, while the employer can try to organize weight loss
competitions or smoking cessation programs, nobody has much incentive
to participate because it may not save them any money, and the employer
may not have much incentive to organize them because it is not getting any
discount for providing these programs. So while the employer may save
money by terminating health insurance as an employee benefit, such a

move may lead to a less healthy workforce, which may cost the employer in productivity down the line.

These are just a few of the reasons many organizations are deciding to continue to offer health insurance to their employees. You may find them convincing; you may not. The important thing is that you take these reasons, and others that you may discover, into account when weighing the very important questions of whether it is in your organization's best interests to offer health insurance or end the benefit.

TAKE AWAY POINTS

- There are several good reasons to continue to offer health insurance, even with the "free year" the Employer Mandate delay appears to offer.
- Penalties for failing to offer insurance or offering low-quality insurance are not tax deductible like premiums.
- "Savings" from dropping coverage will very rarely be as large as the employer expected.
- Attracting and retaining talent will be much easier if the employer offer health insurance.
- Employee relations could be frayed if insurance is dropped.
- Offering insurance allows the employer to have a more direct opportunity to influence workforce wellness, thus protecting against future losses of productivity due to employee health issues.

ACTION ITEMS

- Know your tax rate, and thus, the true cost of the penalties on your business.

- Consider whether your business has key employees who would likely leave if your company ended its health insurance plan while a competitor still offered coverage. Alternatively, consider whether you could attract talented employee of a competitor should they stop offering health insurance.
- Think about the worst-case employee relations scenario that could arise from ending coverage and weigh that against the money saved.
- Take stock of the wellness programs your company presently offers and consider whether more could be implemented.

<u>NOTES</u>

_____

_____

_____

_____

Chapter 6 – Forget Full Time Equivalent, How Do We Determine Who is Full Time and Get them Enrolled?

When we discussed the calculation to determine if an employer is subject to the mandate, a few readers probably said "yeah, yeah, this is great, but I don't even know how to count the number of full time employees at this company, much less my full time equivalents." You may have workers with variable hours, seasonal workers, project employees, and otherwise high turnover. If that is you, then you're in luck, because this chapter is for you. If that is not you, well, you also need to know how to calculate if someone is full time, so this chapter is for you, too.

Variable Hour Employees

Often workers will work a large number of hours in a short period of time for a specific project, and then work sparingly until needed again. For the time they are working, they would certainly be considered "full time;" but would not be full time during the period between jobs. How is an employer supposed to determine if they count in the various Employer Mandate calculations?

Look Back/Measurement Period

In an effort to solve this problem this year, the law creates what is called a "Look Back Period" or "Measurement Period" for employers to total how many hours variable hour employees worked in a certain time period and divide that number by the number of weeks in that period. If the result is greater than 30 per week, that employee is considered full time and must be offered insurance.

The employer gets to choose the length of the Look Back Period, which can be anywhere from three months to twelve months. Employers should work with their brokers or consultants to set the length of the Look Back Period that will minimize the number of employees eligible for coverage, if that is their goal.

Administrative Period

At the conclusion of the Look Back/Measurement Period, an employer can have an Administrative Period of up to ninety days to make arrangement for coverage and get every eligible employee enrolled in a health insurance plan offered by the company. However, the existence of the administrative period may not create coverage gaps for employees already enrolled in an insurance plan provided by the employer.

Stability Period

At the conclusion of the Administrative Period, the employer must have a Stability Period during which time all employees that were deemed to be full time as measured in the Look Back/Measurement Period must be offered qualifying health insurance (coverage that is not too costly and of sufficient quality) to avoid the penalties under the Employer Mandate.

The Stability Period must be at least the longer of a) six months, or b) the length of the Look Back/Measurement Period. For example, if an employer uses a three-month Look Back Period, the Stability Period must be six months. However, if the employer uses a nine-month Look Back Period, the Stability Period would be nine months. The employer is permitted to add a month to the length of the Stability Period, so if the employer used a nine month Look Back Period, they could use a ten month Stability Period.

Going forward, the Stability Period will be the Measurement Period for the employees subject to it. Additionally, different classes of employees (salary v. hourly, collectively bargained v. non-union, etc.) can be subject to different Stability Periods. Human Resource departments are quickly learning the different tools at their disposal to make these calculations. If your organization does not have a Human Resources Department, ask your broker or consultant for help.

Seasonal Employees

But what if a company has college kids who work over the summer, or a store needs extra help around the holidays? Seasonal employees are not variable hour employees, but it wouldn't be fair to have to count them as full time employees. The law makes a provision for that, sort of.

Workers who are employed less than one hundred and twenty days in a year are classified as "Seasonal Workers." Employers need not include "Seasonal Workers" in their Employer Mandate calculations. However, if an employer is subject to the Employer Mandate, it must offer ALL employees access to insurance on their 91st day. Thus, employers must offer seasonal employees health insurance after ninety days, even if that employee will be employed for less than a month after being offered.

Auto-Enrollment

Once an organization has determined who qualifies for coverage as a full time employee, it needs to get them enrolled. If the organization is over two hundred employees, enrollment must be automatic (after the ninety-day waiting period, of course.) During this period, the employee has the ability to opt out of coverage. If they don't and the company is complying with the law, they will automatically be enrolled in the company's health plan on their ninety-first day of work.

TAKE AWAY POINTS

- To determine if variable employees are "full time," an employer measures the hours employees work during a "Look Back Period" of between three and twelve months.
- After the Look Back Period, an employer can take up to ninety days to educate its workforce about insurance options and enroll them during an "Administrative Period."
- After enrolling employees, the employer must permit employee's coverage to all employees who qualify as "full time" for the "Stability Period," which is the longer of six months or the length of the measurement period.
- Seasonal employees, those who work less than 120 days in a year, need not be included in Employer Mandate calculations, but must be offered insurance if they work more than ninety days.
- If a company has more than two hundred employees, the company must have the ability to automatically enroll employees if they do not opt out in their first ninety days of employment.

ACTION ITEMS

- Determine if you have variable hour employees that will require the application of Look Back, Administrative, and Stability Periods.
- Discuss the most favorable measurement period with your human resources department or insurance broker.
- Craft a plan to deal with Seasonal Employees.
- Make sure your organization has an automatic enrollment program in place.

NOTES

_____

_____

_____

_____

Chapter 7 – Changes to the Alphabet Soup of Health Related Employee Benefits

Flex Spending Accounts (FSAs), Health Savings Accounts (HSAs), Health Reimbursement Accounts (HRAs), it is hard to keep track of what most companies even offer anymore, much less changes to them brought on by PPACA. However, the law and subsequent regulations have significantly altered what can be done with these benefits, and attempting to use them "the old way" could lead to significant tax issues for employees.

Flex Spending Accounts

Several companies offer Health FSAs for employees to cover item such as prescriptions and co-pays. An employee simply puts pre-tax dollars into an account and uses that money for out of pocket medical expenses. "In the old days," this money could also be used for medical supplies such as bandages, ointments, and over the counter medications. The advantage was that spending $10 on pain medication with pre-tax dollars was the equivalent of spending $12 if the employee's tax rate was 20%.

That gravy train has ended. PPACA almost immediately mandated that only medicines for which the purchaser has a prescription may be purchased with an FSA, causing the purchaser to either get a prescription or pay for the item with post-tax dollars. In addition to limiting what can be purchased with the money set aside in FSAs, PPACA also limited the amount of money individuals can set aside in FSAs. Previously, there have been no limits on the amount that could be set aside in these plans.

Starting to 2013, individuals have been limited to $2500.00 per year, which will be indexed for inflation.

Health Savings Accounts

Health Savings Accounts have been used as a tool to make participation in a high deductible health plan more palatable. A plan participate would trade a higher deductible for lower premiums. Their out of pocket spending would be higher if they needed care, but judicious use of medical resources was encouraged because the account holder would be using their own money on a large portion of their annual medical care.

However, high deductible plans are now essentially barred for small employer (less than 100 employees) and individual plans because these plans must offer coverage greater than or equal to the benchmark plan for the state. Benchmark plans limit deductibles at $2,000/$4,000, and the out of pocket maximums are $6,350/$12,700. These deductibles are approximately one-third of the current average high-deductible health plan deductibles, making high deductible plans less prevalent.

HSAs will still exist and can be useful to pay expenses related to high deductible health plans. The limits that employees can put aside tax-free in 2014 will be $3,300 for individuals and $6,550 for those with family coverage. HSAs still may not be used to pay premiums, but any amount contributed by the employer can be counted towards the "cost-sharing" (out of pocket maximum) of the employer's plan with respect to affordability.

Health Reimbursement Accounts

Health Reimbursement Accounts are arrangements set up by an employer for an employee's benefit that must be funded by employer contributions, not employee withholdings. HRAs are usually not actual accounts, but rather notations of an amount of health care costs for which an employer will reimburse an employee. This gives an employer some certainty with respect to the amount it will pay (and be able to deduct from taxes) for employee health care, and gives the employee a nice benefits of health coverage for which they need not pay.

Under PPACA, amounts made available under an HRA that is linked with an employer plan count for purposes of determining if the plan is of "minimum value" if the amounts are used only for cost sharing and not to pay insurance premiums. Additionally, amounts newly made available under an HRA that is linked with an employer plan are taken into account only in determining affordability if the employee may use the amounts only for premiums or may choose to use the amounts for either premiums or cost sharing. Bureaucrat to English: HRAs, if used properly, can lower your organization's insurance costs.

TAKE AWAY POINTS

- PPACA has significantly limited the benefits of FSAs by prohibiting the purchase of medical supplies and over the counter drugs without a prescription.
- HSAs are less-effective since high deductible health plans will be less prevalent in the post-PPACA environment.
- HRAs can count as first-dollar coverage and be used to offset employer costs.

ACTION ITEMS

- If you currently offer HSAs, discuss whether it still offers some benefit to your employees with your consultant or broker.

- Examine the use of HRAs as first-dollar coverage to soften the blow of rising premiums.

<u>NOTES</u>

_____

_____

_____

_____

Chapter 8 –Those "Exchanges" You Keep Reading About...

If you haven't already heard about the health insurance exchanges in PPACA, first, shame on you for not reading previous chapters more closely; but second, you will soon not be able to avoid them. The Employer Mandate will thrust the exchanges even further into the limelight, as more people may have incentives to enroll in the Individual Exchanges. Additionally, some theorize that the delay of the Employer Mandate will cause more employers to discontinue coverage, resulting in more people in the exchanges.

This is your primer on the theory of exchanges, the structure of PPACA exchanges, and some examples of how they are supposed to work. While there is no way to effectively address all of the issues surrounding these massive entities (they are worthy of several books unto themselves), hopefully this gives you the information you need to intelligently discuss with your broker, consultant, or HR department whether exchanges make sense for your organization.

In the Beginning...

The theory of health insurance exchanges has been around for several decades, and PPACA's supporters gleefully point out that the conservative Heritage Foundation was an early proponent in the 1980s. The goal is to consolidate consumers who may be in individual and small group plans into larger pools to spread risk and increase bargaining power. How to consolidate consumers and use the bargaining power has been an issue of considerable debate and experimentation, but all agree to the basic premise that larger pools with diverse populations will, as a whole, have more leverage to obtain lower rates.

Prior to PPACA, two states had created exchanges using very different methodologies to consolidate consumers: Utah and Massachusetts. Utah's exchange was a "passive" exchange that set up a website allowing consumers to shop for health insurance. When people refer to "Travelocity for health insurance," they are referring to a model like Utah's. The state did not purchase insurance or have much regulation of which plans were offered in the exchange. Its primary goal was putting insurance companies and consumers in the same place to ease the process.

Massachusetts pursued an "active buyer" model that placed the state in the central role instead of a mere facilitator. The state negotiated with insurance companies to sell insurance to the state. The state then turned around and sold the insurance to individuals and businesses through the exchange. The goal in this type of exchange is to leverage the power of the state to obtain the best deals for its consumers.

Who is in Charge Here?

PPACA passed the power to establish and run exchanges to the states, if they chose to accept it. Crafters of the law figured states would be thrilled to retain control over a large portion of their insurance market, especially since the federal government was providing grants to get them up and running. And if a state was unable to get one up and running by October 2014 or for some reason refused, the federal government would operate an exchange in that state. They figured only a few states would refuse to operate an exchange or be unable to establish one on time. They appear to have miscalculated.

As of June 2013, twenty-seven states are refusing or unable to establish and operate exchanges. Additionally, seven states could not establish an exchange on their own and entered into agreements with the federal government to jointly operate exchanges. Only sixteen states and the District of Columbia will operate their exchanges without federal government assistance. This massive, unexpected undertaking has caused federal guidance regarding the exchanges to be released slower than expected, but we know enough about them to discuss their general set up and what benefits they may offer employers.

How Do They Work?

There are two types of exchanges established by PPACA: the Individual and the Small Business Health Options Plan ("SHOP"). The SHOP exchanges impact employers directly; and while the Individual exchanges have a less direct effect, their potential impact is just as great. Whether an exchange is more like Utah or Massachusetts varies by state, but to say most are somewhere in between the two is a safe answer.

SHOP Exchanges are designed to make insurance more affordable for businesses with (generally) less than one hundred employees.[10] If you have been reading this book carefully thus far, you can figure out that SHOP exchanges are meant as a way to keep smaller employers from simply dropping coverage and paying the penalty. The employer can either deal directly with the exchange, with a broker, or with "Navigators" to shop for plans in the exchange without any fluctuation in price.

The plans offered through the exchanges will be different levels of coverage. Bronze plans will have an actuarial value[11] of 60% (the

---

[10] Larger employers will be permitted to join in 2017.

[11] As you may recall, "actuarial value" is close, but not identical, to the percentage

minimum needed to satisfy the Employer Mandate), Silver – 70%, Gold – 80%, and Platinum plans will have an actuarial value of 90%. The goal is for the exchanges to have several plans to choose from at each level. This may not occur initially, but as insurers figure out the risks associated with the groups in the exchanges, they will be more confident and provide more options…at least the exchange operators' hope.

The Individual Exchanges operate in much the same way except the purchaser is an individual instead of a small business. The same metal levels apply and the Exchanges may be accessed directly by the consumer, through a broker, or through a Navigator. These Exchanges are where the law's drafters believed all of the previously discussed Young Invincibles would purchase their insurance instead of paying the Individual Mandate tax. And then there are the tax credits. Lots and lots of tax credits.

Exchange Tax Credits

Sorry, the tax credits available through the SHOP Exchanges are pretty limited and will be discussed in a later chapter. However, the Individual Exchanges throw around tax credits and subsidies like beads at Mardi Gras, and there are plenty for everyone.

Individuals and families with income up to 250% of the Federal Poverty Level (FPL) are eligible for reduced premiums through the exchanges. While the formula is complicated, the most basic (and, admittedly, not absolutely always correct) formula for a Silver plan is: 100%-150% of FPL = Plan will have Actuarial Value of 94% (enrollee pays approximately 6% of the medical costs)

---

of costs covered by the plan. So a plan with a 60% actuarial value covers about 60% of the Essential Health Benefits received by the covered person.

151%-200% of FPL = Plan will have Actuarial Value of 87% (enrollee pays approximately 13% of the medical costs)

201%-250% of FPL = Plan will have Actuarial Value of 73% (enrollee pays approximately 27% of the medical costs)

In addition to these subsidies, individuals and families up to 400% of the FPL can receive tax credits to assist with the costs of purchasing insurance through an exchange. This tax credit is based on the premium for the second lowest cost Silver plan in the exchange in the state where the person is eligible to purchase coverage. The amount of the tax credit varies with income so the premium that an individual or family would have to pay for the second lowest cost Silver plan would not exceed a specified percentage of their income (adjusted for family size), as follows:

Up to 133% FPL = 2% of income

134%-150% FPL = 3-4 % of income

151%-200% FPL = 4%-6.3% of income

201%-250% FPL = 6.3%-8.05% of income

251%-300% FPL = 8.05%-9.5% of income

301%-400% FPL = 9.5% of income

It is important to note income reports are what an individual or family projects they will make for the year in which the credit is provided, instead of what they made the previous year, because the credit is paid at the time the insurance is purchased instead of as reimbursement after the taxpayer has fronted the cost of the premiums.

Employers might be thinking at this point "this is great, all of my employees will just get tax credits through the exchange, get off my books, and I'm home free!" Not so fast. Individuals and families are not eligible for tax credits unless their employer does not offer coverage or the coverage is either unaffordable or of low value. In fact, the event that triggers an employer's penalty is an employee seeking a subsidy in the exchange. So employees can sprint to the exchanges, but if the employer offers qualifying coverage, they will get no financial assistance to purchase insurance, and thus would likely remain on the employer's plan.

This sets up an interesting scenario the law's drafters clearly did not intend and will need to get creative to fix. Imagine if you will a family of four, with one individual working, making 200% of the FPL for a family of four ($47,100). As you may recall, coverage is "affordable" if the employee is offered *individual* insurance at the Bronze-level (60% actuarial value) for no greater than 9.5% of household income; in this case, $4,474.25. However, if that employee were eligible for a tax credit, that same employee could be guaranteed to pay no more than $2,967.30 for *family* coverage, and would only pay 13% of qualifying medical expenses in a Silver-level plan, instead of 40% through the employer plan. Thus, the employer offering qualifying coverage costs the employee over $1500 plus the cost of insuring the rest of their family, plus 27% in the actuarial value of the plan, all to avoid the Employer Mandate penalty. This unintended consequence is something to discuss with your broker or consultant when charting your path forward.

Astute readers are thinking "hey, didn't he say employer reporting was delayed until 2015? So how will the IRS verify that someone is eligible for a tax credit in 2014?" It can't and it won't. The regulations relating to the exchange tax credits tell the states operating the exchanges to accept the taxpayers "self-reporting" of eligibility as sufficient. Yes. Tax credits will be given out on an "honor system." This has caused some analysts to assume that some ne'er-do-wells will participate in the Individual Exchanges and improperly receive tax credits. While this will drive up the cost of the law, it will also bolster a key element the government needs to be successful for the law to work as hoped.

TAKE AWAY POINTS

- The goal of health insurance exchanges is to get individuals and businesses previously fending for themselves into larger pools so the risk can be spread and premiums lowered.
- Utah and Massachusetts are the polar opposite pre-PPACA examples of exchanges, with Utah simply establishing the marketplace while Massachusetts actually purchased the insurance from insurers and sold it to consumers.
- Twenty-seven states either refused or were unable to establish an exchange in the time allotted by the federal government. Thus, the federal government will operate exchanges in those states. Additionally, seven states need to federal government's help.
- SHOP exchanges are for businesses with 100 or fewer employees. Individual exchanges are for families and individuals who either do not have employer sponsored coverage or whose employer sponsored coverage is either unaffordable or of low quality.
- Tax credits and subsidies are available in the Individual exchanges if the person seeking the credit or subsidy was not offered qualifying insurance by their employer. For 2014, exchanges are to rely on an "honor system" whereby they will accept the employee's claim of eligibility without the ability to verify by checking employer reporting.

ACTION ITEMS

- Investigate whether your state is operating its own exchange or is deferring to the federal government.
- Determine if your organization would be eligible to participate in your state's SHOP exchange. If so, ask your broker or consultant to obtain a quote for coverage through the exchange.
- When performing your calculations to determine if your company comes out ahead if it drops insurance, try to factor in the costs to employees of family coverage if your organization does provide qualifying coverage.

NOTES

_____

_____

_____

_____

Chapter 9 – Other Provisions Impacting Employers

You didn't think you were finished, did you? There are so many changes in this law, it is almost impossible to identify all that will impact employers in some way, because even those not directly related to employer plans will cause alterations to the structure and pricing of plans. Here are some of the additional obligations employers face and important provisions impacting the health insurance market.

Medical Loss Ratio

PPACA's Medical Loss Ratio (MLR) rules took effect in 2012, requiring insurers to spend either eighty-five or eighty percent (depending on the type of plan) on actual medical costs. Thus, they may only spend up to fifteen or twenty percent of the premiums received on administrative costs such as marketing, enrollment costs, and claims administration. If they spend a higher percentage on administrative costs, they must provide a rebate to the plan's participants in the amount of the rebate. For example, if an insurer is permitted to spend fifteen percent of a certain plan's premiums on administrative costs and they spend seventeen percent, they must send a refund to the plan participants in an amount equal to two percent of the premiums collected.

But, of course, sending it directly to the plan participants would be too easy, wouldn't it? Insurers may send the rebates to the organization providing the plan to its employees, who must then distribute the rebates to the plan participants. While there was much confusion regarding how this could be done without upsetting the ERISA apple cart or drawing the ire of the IRS, most brokers and insurers can advise plan sponsors (employers) how to efficiently distribute the rebate. The 30,000 foot view for employers is to devise a fair plan that does not favor the people running the plan and do its best (but doesn't need to go to extreme lengths) to provide rebates to plan participants from the previous year who are no longer employed by the organization. While I certainly cannot speak to Department of Labor and IRS enforcement priorities, I cannot imagine they will dedicate many resources to prosecuting companies that try to distribute the rebates in good faith.

By the way, MLR is one of the reasons many employers with high turnover find it difficult to offer insurance in the post-PPACA environment. Fast food restaurants and retailers have such turnover that the administrative costs of constantly adding and subtracting people from the plans sometimes approaches 40%. Additionally, these employers traditionally employ workers who cannot afford premiums for full health plans, but want catastrophic coverage for emergencies and serious illnesses. These plans were called "Mini-Med" plans, but do not satisfy PPACA Essential Health Benefits and cost-sharing requirements, and do not come close to satisfying MLR.

Summary of Benefits and Coverage

Plan sponsors (employers) are also required to provide plan participants (employees) with a summary of the health insurance offered, and, as you can imagine, the law is pretty darn specific about how it must look and what information it must contain. Willful failure to comply with this requirement can lead to a penalty of $1000 per violation per day.

Fortunately, insurance companies have already mastered how to draft these summaries and would look really silly if one of their insureds was fined. However, be sure you receive these, and make sure your broker or consultant is on top of getting you to distribute them at the various prescribed times.

W-2 Reporting

Very large employers (over 250 employees) must provide the total cost of employer-sponsored health insurance, paid by both employer and employee, on employees' 2012 W-2. Without further exemptions, all employers will be required to provide the information on 2013 W-2s and beyond. This is informational only, and neither the employer nor employee has any real action that can be taken as a result of this information.

Notice of Exchange Rights

Starting October 1, 2013, employers are required to provide employees with notice of their rights in the health insurance exchanges. The notice must inform employees about the existence of the health benefits exchange and explain how the employee may be eligible for a premium tax credit or a cost-sharing reduction if the employer does not offer coverage or offers coverage that is unaffordable or of low quality. The notice also need to inform employees that if they purchase insurance through the exchange, they may lose any employer contribution toward the cost of employer-provided coverage, and the tax consequences of such a decision. Lastly, the notice must include contact information for the exchange, and an explanation of appeal rights.

The Department of Labor has model language on their website for both employers that offer insurance that those that do not. Obviously, if an employer shares language provided by the Department of Labor, the likelihood of success of any claim that the employer failed to comply with the requirement is pretty low.

New Taxes on Insurance Companies

While employers are not directly responsible for three new taxes on insurance companies, understanding of very basic business principles, history, and insurance companies' own statements demonstrate that insurance companies will pass these additional costs onto customers. The first is a $1-2 dollar charge on every plan to research the comparative effectiveness of medical treatments. OK, simple enough. The cost of every plan will increase by $1-2. Somehow I think plan sponsors will survive this cost.

The second will have a much larger impact on premiums. In 2014, insurance companies will be required to pay, as an industry, an $8 billion "Health Insurance Industry Fee." The fee increases annually until it reaches $14.3 billion in 2018. For some perspective, the private health care industry in America is estimated to create revenue of $750-$850 billion per year. The average margin of companies in the industry is estimated to be between 3.5-5%. If these numbers are correct (and, as you can imagine, finding neutral, citable industry-wide numbers is difficult), the health insurance industry's total profit is between $26.2-42.5 billion. Would your industry take a tax hit that eventually eats up somewhere between 33-50% of your profit instead of passing that onto customers? I didn't think so.

The third fee is a three-year "Reinsurance Assessment" of $12 billion in 2014, $8 billion in 2015, and $5 billion in 2016. The "per enrollee" fee has been set at $63 for 2014. Thus, the cost of each plan will necessarily increase by at least $63 in 2014.

TAKE AWAY POINTS

- There are several other changes that will impact employers, and more are created by regulations every month.
- Medical Loss Ratio requires insurance companies to spend a certain percentage of premiums collected (80% or 85%) on actual medical services instead of administrative costs, and must rebate plan participants if they fail to meet that percentage.
- Employers must provide Summaries of Benefits and Coverage to employees. Fortunately, insurers are providing compliant documents without must difficulty.
- Employers with over 250 employees must list the total amount of employer-sponsored coverage on employees' W-2.
- Employers must post a notice informing employees of their rights in the health insurance exchanges.
- New taxes will impact the cost of insurance.

ACTION ITEMS

- If you haven't already, make sure you have a plan for distributing Medical Loss Ratio rebates to employees.
- Make sure your insurer is providing you with a Summary of Benefits and Coverage.
- If you have over 250 employees, work with your human resources department or payroll company to include the cost of employer-sponsored coverage on employees' W-2s.
- Provide employees with the notice of exchange rights provided by the Department of Labor.

- Be alert for news of new fees and taxes on insurance companies and plans, and understand that those increases will be added to the cost of your plan.

NOTES

_____

_____

_____

_____

SECTION 3 - OPPORTUNITIES AND STRATEGIES

Chapter 10 – Tax Credits and Wellness Programs

PPACA contains several provisions that are intended to lessen the strain on small businesses of the provisions applying upward pressure on premiums. The most direct are tax credits, but, as you will see, these are difficult to obtain. A much easier, and possibly more beneficial means for everyone, are wellness programs that reward both employees and employers for changing unhealthy behaviors.

Small Business Tax Credit

If an organization employs less than twenty-five employees and pays an average salary or less than $50,000.00, it may be able to claim a tax credit if it also pays at least 50% of the health care premiums in an employer sponsored plan. For 2013, for-profit employers can receive a maximum credit equal to 35% of their contributions, while non-profit employers can receive a maximum credit up to 25%.

The maximum credit is available to an employer with ten or fewer employees who make an average of $25,000.00 or less, with all premiums paid by the employer. From that point, the credit phases out until an employer with 24 full-time employees averaging $50,000.00 receives up to a 2% credit towards whatever percentage of employer premiums it paid. The IRS has created a calculator that allows employers to enter information to determine if they qualify, and to what level.[12]

---

[12]The Internal Revenue Service, Taxpayer Advocate Service, *Small Business Health Credit Tax Credit Estimator*, available at: http://www.taxpayeradvocate.irs.gov/calculator/SBHCTC.htm (last visited July 17, 2013).

Got it? Didn't think so. Here are a few questions to ask, and some examples of how the credit works. First, do you employ less than 25 full time equivalent employees? Owners and their family members (including nieces, nephews, cousins, etc.) do not count. Second, do you pay an average wage of less than $50,000.00? Third, do you pay at least 50% of the premiums for your employees' health insurance through a group plan? If you answered "yes" to all of these questions, you are you are eligible to receive a tax credit of between 2-35% of the premiums you paid. You will need to find your organization's spot on the phase out charts to determine exactly how much of a credit you will receive.

For example, if an employer with 10 employees who average $25,000.00 in salary pays 100% of the premiums for these employees' coverage, which we'll say totals $100,000.00, that employer is eligible for a $35,000.00 tax credit. In 2014, the maximum credit for for-profit employers increases to 50% (35% for non-profit employers), so this employer would be eligible for a $50,000.00 tax credit. An employer with 24 employees making an average of $50,000.00 that is covering 50% of the employees' premiums will get a credit of 2% of what it paid, which will result in a 1% tax credit. Thus, the value of this credit varies immensely, so working with a broker or accountant is essential in determining if an organization can benefit for it.

In addition to the increase in the size of the credit in 2014, an employer will be also be required to purchase insurance in the SHOP exchange to be eligible for the credit, even with the delay to the Employer Mandate. The law's drafters hope this will be yet another reason for small businesses to pool together in the exchange.

Wellness Grants

PPACA authorizes $200 million for employers to establish wellness programs intended to fight certain chronic ailments like diabetes and obesity. They were supposed to be available between September 2010 and September 2015, but were not rolled out by the Center for Disease Control as the National Healthy Worksite Program until 2012. Employees must submit proper forms, and be sure to hire a wellness program coordinator who can provide a return on investment calculator. To be honest, these grants are difficult to obtain and keep, so most employers interested in lower rates through a healthier workforce will save a lot more money with:

Wellness Programs

Under ERISA, a plan sponsor (employer) may only reward an employee for positive behavior in the amount of 20% of the employee's contribution. Under PPACA, employers may incentivize employees to participate in wellness programs up to 30% of their contribution. Additionally, employers may impose a 50% penalty/reward for tobacco use. The reward is tied to the plan's minimum value and will give the employer more flexibility with their plan design.

For example, imagine an employer-sponsored group health plan has an annual premium of $6,000, split $4500 employer/$1500 employee and offers employees a health-contingent wellness program focused on exercise, weight and blood pressure. The reward for compliance is an annual premium rebate, not to exceed $1,800, which is 30 percent of the total annual cost of employee-only coverage ($6,000 x 30 percent = $1,800). Now imagine the wellness program is exclusively for tobacco-prevention. Employees who have used tobacco in the last 12 months and who are not enrolled in the plan's tobacco cessation program are assessed a premium surcharge in addition to their employee contribution toward the coverage. The surcharge must not exceed $3,000, which is 50 percent of the total annual cost of employee-only coverage ($6,000 x 50 percent = $3,000).

Pretty simple, right? OK, just realize that they are out there, they can make your workforce healthier, and there is a cottage industry of bright people creating great programs that insurers and brokers can match with the right organizations.

TAKE AWAY POINTS

- The Small Business Tax Credit allows businesses employing less than twenty five people at an average salary of less than $50,000.00 to receive a tax credit of up to 35 % of the employer's contribution.

- The tax credit increases to 50% of the employers' contribution in 2014, but the coverage must be purchased in the employers' state SHOP Exchanges, even though the Employer Mandate is delayed a year.

- Wellness grants are available.

- A more likely means of helping a workforce become healthier are wellness incentive programs, which can now provide credits/penalties of up to 30%, with a possible 50% penalty/credit for tobacco use.

ACTION ITEMS

- Work with an accountant to determine if your organization is eligible for a Small Business Tax Credit under PPACA.
- Work with your broker or insurer to design a wellness program that fits your organization's group plan makeup. There is no good reason to refuse to at least allow your broker or insurer to research options that could save you and your employees money.

NOTES

_____

_____

_____

_____

Chapter 11 – Changing The Entire Plan Design

With such drastic changes to the health insurance market taking place, some employers are deciding to make drastic changes themselves. Some are experimenting with defined contribution plans to guarantee costs, while others are finding that self-insurance, once only reasonable for larger employers, may be an option for them.

Defined Contribution

Employers facing a competitive labor market and an uncertain insurance market are searching for some cost certainty, and some are finding it with defined contribution plans. These plans, in contrast to traditional defined benefits that prescribe a set of benefits, provide a certain amount of money to an employee's cafeteria plan or HRA to purchase coverage. While putting money into an HRA with which employees can purchase insurance does not satisfy the Employer Mandate, there may be ways to arrange benefits packages to achieve both.

Employers can offer a plan that satisfies the Employer Mandate, but is not as attractive as individual plans an employer is able to offer to its employees. Finding an insurer that will offer an employer plan with an expected very low participation rate could be a challenge, so working with a broker or consultant that has developed a system will be essential to successfully switching to a defined contribution model.

Self-Insuring

Companies that self-insure put money in a fund, and then usually hire a third-party administrator to deal with claims, cutting out insurance companies by paying all of the medical bills themselves. They are essentially the insurance company for their enrollees. This gives the employer much more control over costs, and allows them to set benefits in a manner that is most beneficial to their enrollees.

Self-insuring has traditionally been limited to larger companies that could afford the hit of several bad incidents in a year. Due to the higher premiums occurring as a result of PPACA and additional regulations, the threshold of the size at which self-insurance makes sense may be lowering; but only if the company fully understands the significant risks associated with this strategy. There are also groups of employers that form entities that allow them to self-insure multiple companies in the same risk pool.

Several companies that market self-insured plans are entering new markets, selling self-insurance as a hedge against potential premium increases and regulatory requirements. Self-insured plans are not subject to the Health Insurance Industry Tax, nor must they comply with Essential Health Benefits, Community Rating, Guaranteed Issue, and Medical Loss Ratio. Over half of all Americans enrolled in employer-sponsored plans are in self-insured plans. Why isn't everyone?!

Three words explain why self-insured plans do not make sense for everyone: NO ANNUAL LIMITS. Prior to PPACA, a company could take comfort in the fact that each medical incident had a "worst case scenario" limited to the annual limit for the plan, or the lifetime limit if the issue was ongoing. There are no limits now, so there is no way to know what the company's "worst case scenario" might be. In a group of 60 participants with average health histories, three large medical incidents (cancer, debilitating injury, etc.) could be devastating to the company's financial health. The plan needs to be of a size sufficient to absorb the blows of multiple large claims at one time. If a smaller group has set aside an amount equal to 100% of the previous year's claims, bad events forcing that amount up to 130% or higher of the previous year's claims could ruin the company.

One means of minimizing the risks associated with self-insured plans is to purchase "stop-loss" coverage that takes over as the primary insurer once the self-insured plan has paid a certain percentage of expected claims. For example, a company could get stop-loss coverage for all claims over 115% of the previous year's claims. Thus, the company would only be responsible for 15% more than it was expecting to cover. Be careful, however, as stop-loss coverage is regulated by state insurance commissions, and the rules regarding their use vary widely. Additionally, some stop-loss plans cover a range of losses, say 115%-125%, and then the employer is back on the hook. Before jumping on the self-insured bandwagon, be sure to thoroughly discuss the plan with a trusted insurance consultant or broker.

TAKE AWAY POINTS

- Defined Contribution plans give employees a set amount they may apply to benefits instead of providing them with a defined list of benefits in a traditional plan.
- Providing employees money through an HRA with which they can purchase individual plans does not satisfy the Employer Mandate.
- It may be possible to offer insurance through a group plan (thus satisfying the Employer Mandate) and also offer to provide money to purchase individual coverage. This is complicated, so be sure to work with an experienced consultant, broker, and/or attorney.

- PPACA has made self-insuring more tempting, but the ban on annual and lifetime limits should cause most employers to pause before establishing such a plan.

ACTION ITEMS

- Discuss the feasibility of transferring to a defined contribution plan with your consultant or broker.
- If self-insuring seems like an option that might make sense for your organization, work very closely with a trusted and experienced consultant or broker to ensure you're your organization does not take on more risk that it can reasonably handle.

NOTES

_____

_____

_____

_____

SECTION 4 – GAZING INTO THE CRYSTAL BALL

Chapter 12 – Landmines and Legal Challenges

Now that we've learned what the law is *trying* to do, let's take a moment to play the pessimists and address some of the issues this law still faces on its path to full implementation. As previously discussed, the Employer Mandate ran into too many obstacles to avoid delay, and the impact of that delay has broad reach to the rest of the law. There are several other potential market forces and legal actions that can trip up other aspects of the law if those implementing are not careful...or even if they are.

What if You Build It, But They Do Not Come?

Everyone has seen (or should immediately see) the 1989 film *Field of Dreams*, in which Kevin Costner's character decides to build a baseball diamond in his corn field after hearing a constant whisper of "if you build it, they will come." In the end, of course, he built it, and they came. [13] But what if they didn't?

A similar question should be asked about the health insurance exchanges. What if very few businesses participate in the SHOP exchanges and less individuals than expected dive into the Individual Exchange risk pools? Or worse yet, what if the only groups that join the SHOP exchanges and only people in the Individual Exchange are not the Young Invincibles, but rather the riverside home owners. [14] This risk of

---

[13] OK, OK, the actual quote is "If you build it, he will come," but has been transformed into the quote above through popular culture and, quite frankly, it much more effectively makes the point.

[14] If you skipped straight to this chapter, please read Chapter 3 to understand this reference.

adverse selection, either by only unhealthy employer groups entering the SHOP exchange or healthy individuals sitting out of the Individual Exchange, has been known for some time. The Obama Administration has dedicated significant resources to promoting the exchanges and attracting a healthy pool through tax credits and subsidies (which, as discussed below, are subject to legal challenges). If only the unhealthy enter the exchanges, insurance companies will be unlikely to continue offering their plans through the exchanges, and states (or the Federal government) will be left with a pool of less than desirable consumers[15] to find coverage for, and no guarantee that they can be transferred to Medicaid because many states have decided not to participate in the expansion.

Of course, they could be wildly successful. They could be moderately successful. They could achieve the most average amount of success any health insurance exchange has ever seen. All of these would justify their existence; but failure of the exchanges would be a real blow to the overall success of the law.

What About Those Rascally Healthy Law Breakers?

Remember those Young Invincibles and the possibility of them not purchasing insurance until needed? That is a very real possibility, and a very real threat to the success of the law. As we previously discussed, the cost of paying the Individual Mandate tax will likely be less than the cost of premiums for many Young Invincibles. And since Guaranteed Issue and Community Rating will be in effect (no pre-existing conditions, regardless of how recent), they can buy coverage on the way to the ER. If they or anyone who does not need health care immediately sits out until

---

[15] From a purely health insurance underwriting perspective. I am sure most are absolutely delightful people.

coverage is needed, the only time new premium revenues will come in is when new claims are filed. That, obviously, is not sustainable.

There may be ways to prevent this, but they would be difficult to implement and run counter to the purposes behind the law's policies. Regulations could permit insurance plans to include a "waiting period" after purchasing insurance before a claim can be made. What if someone applies for coverage without the intention of receiving immediate care, but then is in a terrible accident immediately before the waiting period expires and needs extensive care? Do you deny them? Thus, an effective waiting period policy would necessarily contain exceptions and situational allowances.

There could also be "enrollment periods" for coverage and, if someone did not purchase coverage during that period, they could either be denied coverage, a waiting period could be imposed, or some other undesirable penalty could be imposed. Supporters of this theory point to Medicare enrollment periods as proof this idea can work. However, Medicare enrollment is automatic at age 65 and a recipient remains eligible until their death. There are very few life events than can trigger need or lack of need of coverage. For individuals and families, they may be enrolled in a health plan, then lose a job outside of the enrollment period. Or someone may lose coverage due to non-payment outside of the enrollment period, then attempt to re-enroll. There is also the fact the plans are purchased from private insurers in the private market, instead of insurers who contract with the government to operate within a government program, as is the case with Medicare. Would the public think kindly of government telling a private company when they are permitted to enter into a contract with a private individual?

How Would They Know?

The law's implementers have stated that the Individual Mandate will still take effect January 1, 2014. However, if the employer and insurer reporting is not in effect in 2014, how will the IRS know who is failing to comply with the Individual Mandate? Sure, self-reporting is in effect, but couldn't a person claim that their employer did not offer qualifying coverage, and the IRS would have no way of knowing if this were true? This is not raised by commentators to teach people how to game the system, but rather to point out a flaw that will hopefully be addressed.

These are just a few of the potential market-based problems the law may encounter in the near future. Several others are raised primarily by political partisans, but discussing those in too much detail would violate the "not an op-ed" promise of the Introduction.

Legal Challenges

Even after receiving a tentative blessing from the Supreme Court, various provisions of the law still face challenges. Some would have large effect on the purposes of the law, some small, but all are far from resolved.

First, several states and business owners in states in which the Federal government will operate exchanges (because the state was either unwilling or unable to establish one itself) are challenging the possible assessment of penalties relating to the Employer Mandate. The plaintiffs' theory is that PPACA allows the IRS to provide tax credits to individuals who purchase insurance through state exchanges. To pay for these credits, the IRS is permitted to charge non-compliant employers with the Mandate penalty. However, the legislation does not explicitly permit the IRS to provide subsidies to residents of states in which the Federal government operates an exchange. Accordingly, the law does not permit the IRS to charge the Mandate penalty to employers in states that will have an exchange operated by the Federal government. A few of the law's drafters commented before the law was passed that this difference was intended as a carrot/stick to incentivize states to establish exchanges. However, the IRS claims the difference was not intentional, and they are permitted to provide credits and charge the Mandate penalty in all states, regardless of whether the state or Federal government operates the exchange. If these lawsuits are successful, tax credits to purchase insurance in the exchange would be unavailable in twenty-seven states. Obviously, this would be a huge blow to the law's effectiveness in getting people covered through exchanges.

Next, the law's mandate that all health plans provide contraceptive services is being challenged by religious organizations and employers as a violation of their right to practice their religion. While the Administration has attempted to soften the impact of this provision on religious organizations, the religious organizations hold that any level of contribution to contraception violates their freedom. These lawsuits are in the early stages, but might reach the Supreme Court in the next year or two.

Third, assume there will be several avenues of attack relating to the delay of the Employer Mandate. Employees who lose coverage may have standing to question whether the Executive Branch has the ability to delay the Mandate without Congressional approval.

Finally, there will surely be several other actions that arise as the law takes effect, but need to be brought as "as applied" challenges. Some issues that will almost certainly be litigated include IRS challenges to company break-ups, business challenges to certain applications of the Employer Mandate, actions alleging the Executive branch has overstepped its Constitutional boundaries in regulation writing, and fights over the calculation of full-time equivalent or full-time employees in complex situations. Of course, there are dozens of other possibilities, but many cannot be known until further regulations are drafted or existing regulations are applied in certain ways. One thing about the challenges is certain: they will not end for quite some time.

TAKE AWAY POINTS

- The law is far from fully implemented, as there are still several rules and regulations yet to be promulgated and clarifications regarding prior rules and regulations needed.
- If healthy groups and individuals stay away from the exchanges, insurers may back out, causing damage to the stability of the exchanges.
- If people opt to pay the Individual Mandate penalty (tax) instead of purchase insurance, and only purchase insurance when they need it, insurance companies will be unable to stay in business.
- The agencies charged with enforcing the law must figure out how to verify Individual Mandate compliance without the aid of employer or insurer reporting.
- There are still several challenges to the law pending, including challenges to the Employer Mandate penalty and contraception mandate.

ACTION ITEMS

- Keep abreast of PPACA implementation in your state to see if any issues impact your organizations.
- If you believe you may have a legal action regarding how PPACA is applied to your organization or are challenged by an agency enforcing PPACA, don't assume you are in the wrong. Contact an attorney to investigate whether you have an action. Remember, this law is new. There is very little settled law regarding its application.

NOTES

_____

_____

_____

_____

Chapter 13 – Fun Facts to Amaze and Astound
Your Friends and Co-Workers

The law has generated so many myths and half-truths, it is impossible to keep track of all of them. From the Obamacare real estate tax (not true in almost all cases) to mandated microchip implantations (absolutely untrue), most are false, but some have a little truth to them. So here are some of the law's oddities that seem rather out of place. There are no Take Away Points or Action Items here, just a fun list of tidbits that will make you the hit of your next PPACA-themed cocktail party.[16]

Tell the Truth

First, it is important to have facts correct, lest you violate the law by spreading lies. The law amends ERISA to make it illegal to "make a false statement or false representation of fact,
knowing it to be false," about a health care plan. OK, so this applies to the marketing and sale of plans, but just to be safe, let's make sure we stay on the right side of the facts.

People Get Sick at Sea, Too

Most people could probably list many governmental bodies that they would think might be involved in the various new Boards and committees created by PPACA. HHS, Labor, Centers for Disease Control, Coast Guard, National Institutes of Health, wait, what?!

---

[16] I'm not the only one who has these, right? Right?!

Yes, the Coast Guard is a member of the Interagency Working Group on Health Care Quality. So next time you see a vessel patrolling the waters, just know that not only can those ladies and gentlemen aboard rescue stranded boaters and keep our waters safe, but they can also analyze the comparative effectiveness of various methods of removing a spleen on the fly. *Semper Paratus*, indeed.

Is My Fishing Pole a Durable Medical Device?

January 1, 2013, a new 2.3% tax on the first sale of a piece of durable medical equipment took effect. However, the rollout could have been smoother, and the law a little more clearly written. It was so confusing that tax software writers included it in 2013 updates, and the tax was charged to a variety of goods that would not typically be considered "durable medical equipment." Most notable of the retailers to charge the tax on everything was the fishing and hunting retailer Cabela's. Sure, there may be a situation where those bullets may prolong your life, but medical equipment they are not.

You're Hired! Let Us Know if You Can't Do Your Work, So We Can Do It For You.

The Independent Payment Advisory Board (IPAB)[17] is charged with the task of drafting an extraordinarily detailed report regarding Medicare payment trends and recommendations. The details of what must be in the report take up several pages of the law's text. It is a monster of a report. But what if they decide it is just a little too much for them? In that case, the Secretary of Health and Human Services must draft the report.

---

[17] Yes, the IPAB of "death panel" fame.

Make sure there is plenty of coffee in the Sebelius household. There could be some long nights ahead.

Who Better to Lecture Our Children on Financial Responsibility?

Large bills often stray off topic and include pet projects of legislators who vote in support of the bill. Some are noble, some are pork; but tacking these riders onto large legislation can get some worthy projects funded where they otherwise would not be deemed important enough to bring up on their own.

One of the riders on PPACA is a program to educate adolescents about financial responsibility to prepare them for adulthood. THE FEDERAL GOVERNMENT IS GOING TO TEACH CHILDREN ABOUT FINANCIAL RESPONSIBILITY. While the all-caps was called upon to stress the previous sentence, please read it again and let it sink in. We are doomed.

Closing Thoughts

Despite the delay to the Employer Mandate, the majority of law is not going anywhere until at least 2017 (when a new President could undo it with the help of a friendly Congress), so you might as well finally get comfortable with its contents. I hope this book has given you the understanding you need to make the right choices about your organization's health insurance future. The fact that you deemed learning more about the law and how it impacts your organization important by buying this book and dedicating the time to read it shows you are engaged with the issue and will be ahead of many who *still* hope it will just go away.

Some details are yet to be fleshed out, and the effectiveness of various elements of the law will only be known after the fact, but knowing about its various moving parts will put you in the best position to roll with any changes that may come. When you combine your knowledge with that of your broker or consultant, accountant, and/or attorney, you will weather this storm and emerge a stronger organization.

Acknowledgements

I would like to extend a sincere thank you to Lori Rejent, Mark Avery, Matt Glenn, Stephen Davis, and Bill Hill for their insightful comments and suggestions. Without them, this book would not have been possible.

ABOUT THE AUTHOR

KEVIN J. REJENT
The Rejent Firm, LLC

Kevin Rejent is an attorney in St. Louis, Missouri with over a decade of health law experience. He formed the Rejent Firm, LLC in 2011 to advise small businesses and insurance brokers how to comply with laws and regulations relating to health care reform, and also assist businesses with litigation and operational matters. He frequently lectures business, insurance industry, and legal audiences regarding the latest developments with PPACA and its related laws and regulations.

Kevin is a graduate of Saint Louis University School of Law and served as an Editor of the Law Review. He is also a proud Sun Devil, as he received his Bachelor of Science in Political Science from Arizona State University.

Kevin and his wife Lori have two daughters, Amelia and Charlotte, and twin boys due very soon. He is a member of the Development Board for SSM Cardinal Glennon Children's Medical Center, and active in the local Chamber of Commerce and city government. When he's not enthralled in the latest proposed seasonal employee calculation regulations or changing diapers, he can be found on a golf course or rooting for his St. Louis Cardinals to win their soon-to-be twelfth World Series title (and really hopes this portion of the bio needs updating very soon.)

He can be reached at krejent@rejentlaw.com, www.rejentlaw.com, or follow him on Twitter @KevinRejent.

www.ingramcontent.com/pod-product-compliance
Lightning Source LLC
Chambersburg PA
CBHW030914180526
45163CB00004B/1826